EIGHTEEN TO EIGHTY

a life sketched in poems

Also by Elsa Corbluth

St Patrick's Night (Peterloo Poets, 1988)
*The Planet Iceland (*Peterloo Poets, 2002)
*The Hill Speaks (*Jurassic Press, 2008)
Out There (Bardic Media, 2010)

Elsa Corbluth has won a number of poetry prizes, including in the Arvon, the National, the Bridport, Cheltenham, Yorkshire, Apricot Gold and Poetry on the Lake (Italy).

Her work has also been read on BBC Radio 3 and 4.

Acknowledgements

Acknowledgments are due to the following publications
in which some of these poems first appeared:

Outposts, Orbis, Xenia, SW Review, Gallery, Word and Action, South, Samphire, Poetry Digest, Marshwood Vale Magazine.

Bathing by Candlelight won the poetry Society's A.V. Bowen Prize for a lyric Poem. Part of "Ball in River" was read on Radio 4.

Many of the seasonal poems formed part of the Chesil Poets' (*Word and Action*) programmes of public poetry performed at various venues.

Cover design - Ged Duncan. 'Elsa Today' photo - Vanessa Young.

To David

First Edition 2011

ISBN 978-0-9550605-7-1

Set in Georgia

Published by Bardic Media Ltd
2 Hardy Cottages, School Lane
West Lulworth, Wareham, Dorset BH20 5SA

Printed and bound by Copytech (UK) Ltd
Peterborough

www.bardicmedia.co.uk

St Patrick's Night

Of *Dirge for St Patrick's Night,* from this collection, which won joint first prize in the Cheltenham Prize:

> "I was impressed by the purity and intensity of the emotion expressed." Ruth Fainlight
>
> "...the impersonal voice conveyed deeply personal emotion." Roger Garfitt, *Sunday Telegraph.*

The Planet Iceland

Jack of Clay, from this collection, was shortlisted for the Cheltenham Prize.

> "I kept getting surprised, as much by the form as the content – here a villanelle, there a sonnet, here a tart observation. This is a selection in which 'surprise' would seem to be the key word.' Sam Smith, *The Journal.*

> "Thirty splendid poems jostle for attention. Although many of them are celebrations of her fortune (and tragic misfortune) in family matters, their stance reminds me not of today's mawkish fluffiness in response to personal circumstance, but of the old Norse-nurtured, early Anglo-Saxon poetry of Seafarer or Brunanburg – terse, direct, certainly observant, but never soft-focus." Review by C.J. Heyworth.

The Hill Speaks

> "This accomplished and challenging collection is one where notions of place are reinvested in ways other than the merely lyrically descriptive. The poet is skilled in using conversational, yet at times urgent, tone, imperatives, rhyme and half-rhyme." Joan McGavin, *South.*

About Elsa Corbluth

Elsa has lived in London, Salisbury, Wiltshire, the Lake District, Nottingham and for forty seven years in West Dorset. She left school at fourteen but in her fifties gained a 1st class BA in Combined Creative Arts followed by an MA in Creative Writing.

She has written verse since her earliest years, and won many poetry prizes. She was married for thirty five years and has been divorced for twenty three. Her son lived in Iceland for twenty years and *The Planet Iceland* and *The Hill Speaks* contain several poems on Iceland, drawn from frequent visits there. Her three grandchildren now live with their mother in California.

Her daughter died, aged eighteen, in a fire at the *Kilburn Mother Teresa Hostel for the Homeless,* where she was working as a volunteer. There were no fire precautions in the building. The poetry collection *St Patrick's Night* was an attempt to deal with this.

Eighteen to Eighty

a life sketched in poems

Elsa Corbluth

"Eighteen to Eighty consists of poems not in my other
four collections, and, in contrast to *Out There*
which is not a personal collection, the poems
in *Eighteen to Eighty* are on personal themes.
They also cover many years. The two books could
be companions, the public and the private events
being marked by their dates."

Elsa Corbluth
January 2011

Contents

Eighteen to Eighty – Elsa Corbluth

COLTSFOOT AMONG THE BRICKS
(London, Spring 1948)

Coltsfoot among the bricks,
Hoof of the sun:
Death in the walls left cracks
Where life began.

Spring stabbed with cynic thrust
This weathered rubble:
Unmoved I glanced as though
At fields of stubble.

Warm life the severed crop,
And yet no tragedy
Returns, but leafless hope,
No pain but victory —

Of straight-eyed children,
Tactless as the spring,
Running
Over the bricks and the grass and over
The coltsfoot, sunfoot,
Feet of boys, heavy-shod,
Small boys with earth-smeared faces —

Tall boys with earth-stained eyes
Marching,
Or, earth-forgetful,
Lying,
Their eyes steel,
Earth-conquered:
For death, however ingenious,
Is only death,
And sun and rain know one death,
That is not living.

Coltsfoot among the grass,
Coarse fellside grass,
Sprayed by a river of dust,
Will soon give place

To dandelions, ragwort,
Tawny bracken once
Green, but the gold is not
For us in ravage-rut,
Only the rust, the rot:
No victory but the sun's.

(1948)

SPECTRE DE LA ROSE

Dreaming, she dropped the rose. He, heart of the rose, leapt, whirled and alighted, brought her his hands. Male, full of the summer, bound for the garden, he cannot stay. Earthward, out of the house, she is asleep. Waking, only the rose, and formal daylight.

Dreams and shadows dance, Shadows without substance, hollow trees reflected, Grey ghost-feathers with no swan behind them. Spectre without the rose.

Dreaming, there are no walls. Still, not as stone, swift, not as water, her power is not glacial. Standing as a tree, running as fire her force is volcanic. Night and the snow she knows, but rides them, torch-like.

His eyes are warm. She does not need to turn and meet them. She is looking at the blossom, fire-lit snow, and the swan-down, thistle-puffs of clouds. She knows. Only that he is there, standing a tree-space away. He is in the orchard, among the twisted trunks—twisted apple trees like frozen dancers. He is in the spring.

Who climbs beside her, climbs against the sunset, hooded? Turning, rose-lit, hoodless, gilded: he is on the mountain.

He is the sun and she the earth. He is the sun, not a flame, but the father of flames.

Waking, she is the sea, and he the moon. She gives him back his face and moves in tune with him. In winter she may emulate the earth. Ice-bound she too is solid. But spring brings no blossom, summer no foliage, autumn no fruit. His light is the sun's, her sight the earth's. In the darkness he reflects the sun's heart. She is rolling in the earth's eye-sockets. They shine, but cannot burn.

Unburnt, they leave no ash. No charred woods, scarred heaths, hairless hillsides. No heat-haze, dust-clouds, smoke or thunder-weight. Only the clear unflickering mirrored moon.

Dreaming into the day, wakening at dusk, what is she now? Neither earth nor ocean, swaying in the drunken wind, on the shores of sleep or waking, The sky, dun, neutral as a cygnet's wing, contains both sun and moon. The moon is a threadbare leaf and the sun half an orange skin, rising or setting she cannot tell, having lost her bearings.

She is a forest, green as the sea, brown as the earth, both stiff and loose, both static and changeable, rooted and free, Her conifers bear no petals to fall, no leaves to wither, no flesh-fruits to rot. In this light one cannot mark her limits: borders are blurred...

And whether she stands on the brink of the night or the verge of the day is not known.

(June 1951)

STONE COUNTRY

I

I should be happy, happy in this snow
That cracked the steaming window of the night,
And shocked me into day,
Day on the roofs, day channelling the panes,
And yet my tongue is furred with yesterday.

I should be happy, happy in the hills
That cut the curtains of the afternoon,
Blunt blade of sun that struck my shoulder, black
Boughs that sprang at me, wild geese
In a green sunset, and brass fells.

I should be happy, happy in your love
That threw wide windows of the evening,
Let in the lights, and left no glass to cloud
Before our breathing, gave us all the sky.
I should be happy, happy in your arms,
And yet the walls are green with trickling time.

I was happy at the coming of the snow
In the valley of the coming of the year.
I built a snowman with a tipsy boy:
It leant a little, but its base was strong,
We gave it stones for eyes.
It was my effigy
Carved on tomorrow, and tomorrow threw
Handfuls of rain in its eyes.

I was happy at the coming of your love
On the terrace of the coming of the night.
We went to find the castle on the hill,
And walked, light-limbed, above the blinking town.
We startled trees, we brushed the huddling stones,

We trailed loose fingers in the puddles, lit
Wide eyes of water in the waking town.

II
We have seen
Dawn in the city like a pigeon's wing,
Dawn a grey squirrel in the apple lands,
And dawn like milk,
New milk steaming in the fell-fields, streaming,
Trickling down the cobbles: and a morning
When we missed the dawn.

But I have seen the dying of a dream,
Not yours, not mine,
But I have seen
Love cockle, crackle, curl up, black, smoke-thin,
Float up a chimney, cling and flutter there.

Born of a dying dream, I fluttered too,
Hung in the chimney, dreamed I was alive,
Writhed, reached with withered arms,
Kicked with my crumbling feet,
Wrenched free the frame of me.

Out on the white roof, high above the town,
I thought it was day,
For I had never seen the sun or known
The blue of day.
I smelt the stars,
And the moon froze
My hands, and the clouds caught them.

Out of a drift of ashes, wondering,
You called to me.
I turned, and peering down among the smoke,
I found you green, uncharred.
I spoke to you.

You listened, and my voice came through the wind,
A hammer tapping stone.
I took you with me on the shivering clouds.
I made you king of clouds.

III
But one by one they climbed into the night
Who brought the morning with them in their hair,
The summer in their eyes.
I laughed and clutched the stars.
They pricked my hands,
For they were nettles growing in the dark.

Then one who was all morning looked at me,
Showed me an Arctic summer with no night:
Dazzled I ran with him into the day.
He found my eyes and saw the dawn in them,
He found my hands and felt the spring in them.
I said: my eyes are granite and my hands
Are made for fingering the faults in rock:
He laughed.

But in the window he forgot to laugh.
His chin was tilted at the evening,
His eyes were weighted with the evening;
The evening bit my throat.
Golden, he burned the lashes from my eyes,
His beauty scorched my face.
The evening overflowed, flowed into day,
But in the dawnless morning I forgot.
Laughing, I ran
Over the stubble where a mountain fell,
Flaunting my body's hardness in the sun.
He raced my shadow on the shattered hill.
Resting, he saw
The fine gold threads that lay upon our arms,
But restless, I,

The sharp gold wires that laced the glaciers.
He could not bend my arms.

And in the cold green nausea of return
I hugged the stars,
They cut my breast.
Spray-white, he drained the blood out of my feet:
His beauty chilled my hands.
The sea threw scythes.

I had not known
How his hair was caught behind my eyes,
Or when our teeth had smiled good-bye,
How it would tug at me. I had not known.

IV
Lost in a frowning city, laughterless,
I came to you,
Brought you his eyes, and found they were your own,
Brought you his hair, and found that it was mine.
Your eyes were taut lamps waiting on the bridge,
Watching my hair float underneath like oil.

We walked into the autumn, where the trunks
Felled us with shadows, and the branches bent,
And leaves rocked slowly down. I shook the bark
Out of my hair, and let the morning play.
I gave you apples cold, I gave you dew,
Remembered how to laugh, and called you friend.
You gave me blackberries at noon, warm dust;
But when the sun slipped
Into the hedges, I remembered walls
Built chink on chink to catch the falling sun
In a clenched country,

Remembered brown streams sucking under snow,
Remembered rain,
And knew that I must go
Home to the country I had carved for me,
Home to the self that I had fashioned out of stone.

V

Out on the brown ridge, high above the trees,
I thought it was the spring,
For I had never smelt green bracken, felt
The corn uncoil.
I found the grasses rusting, stones sun-stained,
And found the bones of streams.

Out of the windless city, hungering,
You came to me.
I wedged my hand into a fissure, edged
Across the mountain's chest.
You saw the hill
Open to take me back into its womb:
You saw the mountain bleed.
Because my blood
Was dark beck water, I could feel no pain,
But when it dripped into my eyes, mist hummed:
Stone-pale, you brought the blood back to my hands.
It was your blood I shed.

VI

Night and the lamps swung, strange that I should dream
All the windows melted, all the winds
Waited at the corner of your coming, all my world
Cracked, between the curtains of your arms.

I clung, but I was clinging to a dream,
And two dreams kissed.
My eyes were locked. You thought I was at rest.

My hands were stiff. You thought my pulse was free.
Open your eyes, you said.
You could not see
The cold lights staring in the valley, hear
The cold wind from the mountains crying, feel
The cold road through the passes twisting
Out.
Kiss me, you said.
I tried to free my lips.
Learn, you will learn, you said;
But I had listened to the stars, been trained
By long thin fingers of the mist,
Been scratched by silence.
Too many winters had gone into me,
And I, who cannot, wept.

My tears were cold.
You thought them rain, you thought my blood was warm.
My hair was river weed, my cheeks wet moss,
My eyes were stepping stones into the mist.
You told me I was warm.
My heart was coiled, a snail-shell filled with soil.
You told me I was sane.

But on the glass road I forgot the hills,
Curled in the coat of you so nearly slept,
And through my sexless mountain clothes your hand
Found answer, soft, slow, sure as earth, as age.
I did not understand.

And the stars fell:
We crunched them underfoot, and let the dawn
Into our veins, yes, even into mine.

VII
But when the day swung, squeaking, to its end,
And the wet wheel-wounds of the road lay in between
Your dusk and mine,
My chin dropped on my hand.
I had no hand.
The hand was yours, its fingers stroked my face.
You had no face:
Your hands were tangled in my hair, your hands
Were everywhere
Fear slid,
Fear tunnelled, travelled, waved in front of me,
Fear drummed upon my neck.
I had no self.

Out on the night hill's glimmering crust I pinned
The self I knew.
The hill was opening
The sky was at my feet
And tinfoil stars.
I stooped to touch the sky,
Found knotted ice,
And heard the tinkling of the tinsel reeds.
I found a cavern, combs of icicles
With tottering teeth.
Tadpoles of water slithered down their backs,
And I remembered
The sheep I found upon the sodden fell:
Even the worms inside the skull were dead.

But when your hands came back into the hills
They brought no fear.
They brought the morning with them, brought the snow,
More light than dust of summer on your hair,
For in the sexless mountain night myself
Had answered you
With blood-beats swift, strong, sure as air, as youth,

Yet dared not understand.
I found your ears, your neck,
The space above your eyes,
I found your lips,
And I, who cannot, kissed.
But when the day turned over on its back,
And only spitting coals lay in between
Your dreams and mine,
You felt the pain in me,
You touched its fingertips,
You saw the hands of mist close round my neck:
You saw them part.

I thought that I had drowned.

Out of the mouthless tunnel of the past,
Came, almost into life.

VIII
On to the little snowless fell I led
Myself too new.
The bracken smelt of summer and the wind
Was warm. My tears were warm.
The lichened stones were golden and the day
Was new. My pain was new.
For I, who cannot, loved.

Out of a dream I came. I lived a dream,
But I am tired of dreaming and would live.

And when the rain drips
Loneliness, and when the bells strike
Emptiness, doors swing,
When snow hangs thick brown curtains on the day,
Stars stone, moon sears,
Hills climb each other's backs

To look at me,
And when the wind that should awake me only
Lulls to lethargy,
When the core of the sun is black behind the hills,
And the moon a burned-out match-end in the trees,
Then I would come to you, wind-grazed, star stung,
To rest on you my bare stone-beaten head,
And with the breadth and breath of you defy
All humped and hovering, slumped and lingering things.

IX
Yet keep some part of you
Lest you should find me all
Who had not all,
Lest your warm hands should find my hair frost-glued
Like grass at morning, or your live legs meet
My knees smooth-glazed like paths at evening. Keep
Some self of you.

For I am branded with a burnt-out dream,
Scarred with a scored-out song. For I have loved
Rain in a hollowed rock, for I have kissed
Lips of the corniced snow, have lain to rest
In the arms of the moon.

But in my sleep I groaned.

Love, guard the core of you
Lest you should find
Rock at the root of me.

(1952)

NORTH

What am I to you without the hills?
You asked me.
Darling.
All the ghylls are green with weeping for you,
All the cliffs are stained with seeping
Streams, and all the forest
Stands erect and ready for you,
Cone buds wait,

Wait for you until the rain is clipped,
Until the sun is pulled over the passes,
Until the afternoon,
Glint-stings in bogs, and spat-out cotton grasses,
Until the clouds clap in the evening,
Wait, wait until the night,

Night falling through the rocks,
Rocks round, smooth-skinned,
Night spilt
Into the grizzled moss,
Night dropped like pebbles clinking into tarns,
Night bursting into foam.

Folded inside inside myself you found me
When all the roads were bristling with the frost,
When hills hugged hills and pressed me out between them,
You opened valleys, shook out all the leaves,
Gave me the sun to squeeze, the winds to fondle
What am I without the hills?
I wondered.

Because of you the crags have loosed their fingers
Let me in,
Because of you the fells are open-fisted.

It is because of you that spring is spring,
That I have seen the firm lips of the sun
Draw straight the bracken spirals, seen the sky
Stroking the tarns to sleep, felt air too light
To lift a larch's eyelash, loved
This country.
Yours is a country charred and scarred and spattered,
Sown with broken bottles.
They have bled your grass, your leaves are listless
Lap-dogs' ears,
But here a feline night
Kneads out the day with soft insistent feet,
Breathes rippling into dawn.

And so I told you I would rather lie
And gulp a brown beck burning for you lips
Than thirst upon your lips for taste of stone
Between cramped hedges,
I would rather hold
The ribs of mountains, aching for your breast,
Than hunger, close to you, for points of pines,
Beneath the flaccid fingers of the planes,
Sigh for a twilight frayed with ravens' wings
And sawn with ridges - in a sparrow's dusk

And yet I love you,
Love, I love you:
What are hills,
Hills heaped on hills,
Without you?
All the becks are broken windows smashing
Down the daylight, grinding into darkness,
Clouds are clawed with thunder, crags are crying,
Trees are tortured.

Every day the river twitches,
Every night the stones are throbbing.
What am I without you , who are you
without me,
Darling?

(1952)

WHITE RAIN

White rain shooting, house of rubble,
Windowless and white wind, Why,
Watching the wild geranium beaks
dip, drip,
Am I lonely, loving you, loved?

Bulbs of the rain swell, shiver and hang,
Break as your breath breaks, breaking your dreams.
Rubble flakes fall on your hair and you shiver awake.

White sun spurting, wood of nettles,
Bramble wood, burdock wood. When,
Feeling the wild clematis curls
Stir, shake,
Will you, sun-drops bursting me, break?

(1952)

BATHING BY CANDLELIGHT

Dark mural of myself, big, out of Africa,
Big where the sun drums, slow-swaying woman,
Big for you, woman for you,
Dark in the darkness for you.
Deep
Green for you, gold for you,
Blue in the summer for you,
Taut
Drumskin of earth, I will tap till you loosen,
Tap, let me in, let me through till I find you
Ready where the rain pebbles
Rattle on the earth skin,
Sun bubbles sputter in the thick of the grass.

Live, loved, live with the shadow of me,
Shudder in the leaflight,
Tangled in tree shadows, ready,
I will,
Until the stars suck
Soft, will wait for you
Until the moon pricks through.

(1952)

BACK END

Drone of drugged wasps, hills
A wasp-buzz haze about them,
Yellow days
And damson dusks and damson-dropping nights,
The drystone mornings and the black slug nights
Trailed over cobbled clouds,
And I am ready
To leave these road ends, ridge ends, valley tails,
Dark yellow drowsing hills.

(1952)

MARCH MORNING

Waking to a window of white sky
And whispering birds in pencilled trees
And the thin rustle of rain
I have grown shy
And like a friend new-known I want to say:
Take me, a stranger, strangely to your side
And bring your new face slowly near to mine
To still my racing eyes
And restless ears
With eyes and ears made shy
For meeting me at a new time of year.

(1955)

SUMMER FARM

My tired arms swing free cool tickling drops
Down temples, shoulders, thighs. My body jerks
Dark blots upon blenched ground,
And thick air purrs.
But I have brought my twilight even here
To purple down the haylight?
Or can the knotted earth shake shadows out,
And this sun break me?

Last night there were lovers in the barley.
They left the field dishevelled,
And today the farmer came down early
And, shrugged and grunting, found the stalks all leaning
And criss-cross rumpled.

A thousand nights ago *we* lay together
In a rock-field, when the night was raining,
And in the early day left hand in hand.
There were too many stones to print our sleeping.

Oh sad soft head, how long till fruiting time
Can we endure?
How many years of harvesting dry leaves?

One dayfall shall I, once, come home to you
With straight brown hands,
Cut clean of circling weeds by the wide sun?

Or will my hair blow corn-long in September
When the apple sun is rolling down the sky,
And there be still no reaping?

(1955)

COLOUR BLIND

Shaking along in the dark,
Road black, white rain,
White rails, dark track,
Black sea, white lights half drowned.

Dreams only fill their seas
With jewels: named awake
Their colours break
Into clear glass.
Dreams pour on roads the changing lights of day.

Years through we moved our days
From month to month
In a monotony of white and black
And separately dreamed rich seasons out;

While even black and white
Had rainbows of a thousand greys and darks
If we had only felt the winter in
And slept the flowering summers for our fear.

Put out my dreams and leave me in the dark,
White tears, black room,
And if I write you now in black and white
I'll burn you round with blue!

(1956)

SMALL HOURS

Sea swallowing the sun or sky the moon
And every soft grey river any stone,
All storms the stars
And any pillow tears:
Dear, such a little thing,
If you were every man, I anyone,
Not to remain alone.

(1956)

LEAVES FALLING

At the curling of the year from green,
At the browning of the year,
There will be no burning.

Blue and yellow and brown stick weather;
A whiff of winter.

Somewhere running
Ripples of a different kind of going:
Touch-tingle of a plum
Small-grooved, and sucked-in apple, pushed-out pear,
Bruised tang of air,
Legs in the wet deep grass,
And seeing light combed on water.

Sun-going, and the stacks are yellow-damp.
They are bringing home the rosy cold potatoes.

I will walk the leaves to tatters when the winds
Are swimming in cold water.

All the world through runs a sighing:
Even this year
No puff-throat campions blew fullness in,
But filled their own lips with the summer's blood;
Lion faces of frost-spiked chrysanthemums
Will keep their own proud chins to prick the winter.

I walk as though my hair were grey like creeping smoke,
And start to see sun coloured wisps in puddles.

At the glooming of the year from gold,
At the silver of the year,
Will there be no warming,
Only the turning black of cool sheets in the morning?

(1954)

I TELL YOU

I tell you you must creep
Low in the shivering grass to look for me,
Not where the high hills sleep
Belly to belly with the breathing sky.
For all my dreams of valour I am small.

Though I would string you suns,
Red moons and purple winds
And years of black and gold,
These are my words. My self may only crawl
Where drained leaves lie the summer through
And secret spiders walk their fragile ways.

I tell you I must hide
Deep in the greying woods when thighs of hills
Close on the morning moon,
But follow me,
And though my fingers hang as cold as worms
They will not slide
If you dare circle them as though you held
Your unmade child.

(1956)

SPELLBOUND

The world can get along without my poems
Better than you without my love.
Find me a man of magic who can make
Kisses from commas, lives from golden O's,
For I am tired of conjuring with sounds,
Wand-waving into words
The colour and the liveness of my love.
Find me another sort of sorcerer
Who can undo my half-life's trickery,
And we will pay him my whole world of poems
For one round life without a need of them.

(1956)

FOREST CAROL

1.

Under the bruised sky cringes the bracken.
Christmas trees flicked with frost
shiver, pathetic.
Even the stiff gorse
hunches blunt-prickled where the pale mist blows
like old fine hair around the wrinkled bushes.

Here ghost-white birches, spider-twigged,
the peat-dry puckered elm
and smooth beech bodies licked with bright moss green
in tingling apprehension stand.

Soft in the red-floored cradle of the wood
the god-child lies,
pulsed, glistening, from the dark,
torn, sobbing, to the earth, abandoned there,
a small white strip of pain stretched to the world.

Young nipples of the winter-budded trees
stand proud in wonder.

Who fathered and who bore the white god-child
that cries alone beneath the breath-held trees,
that lies exposed under the wide-eyed sky?

2.

Snug in their yellow-windowed homes
they need not bear,
in their closed rooms, the baby-fingered fear,
nor need they hear
their child's birth agony,

nor walk abroad, until, earth-logged, afraid,
and beaten down by branches, they must kneel
to this born thing
grown from the ugly pallor of their love
to its own loveliness:

Their bodies' white-fire child
that they let fall
for fear it blistered their clay-heavy hands.

3.

It is the time of yellow-lighted joys,
the smoke-blurred jigging time,
puff-bellied daze
and glass-cut laughter,
beer-brown afternoons
and sugared tea-tang times,
nut-cracking jokes,
the slow nights drained of dark
and purple swoon of half-quenched, half-clenched love.

Feast, drink the golden blindness,
curtain your bruised love
and sleep
before the wild white terror overtakes you as you lie.

Wrap him in still brown mist that blots the moon
and fades the sun,
dim down with your bruised dreams
his human limbs.

4.

Under the bruised sky cowers the forest,
green-dark, ragged and monstrous,
and the sun bleeds
to its end in the brute-black wood.

The womb of heaven is great with snow.

(1957)

MIDLAND WINTER

Midwinter midland mope of grey,
Dead gape of sky between
New wet-ink roofs and pit piles serpent-humped.
Oh let the sunlight wave,
Wave down the walls like yellow hair,
And let the sky upturn
Until this frightened landless landscape smiles,

Or light in me, my love, a little sun,
A warm brave yellow cat's eye that will melt
A small hole in the fog.
I will not ask for summer or for love
In storms of rainbow fire,
But for a yellow bead of winter sun
To hold, the grey time through.

Come with me to the breathing breast of earth,
The breast-lips of the tawny winter hills,
The shy close buttocks of the under-fields,
And over all the body's land let grow
Light scribbles of new snow,
As new cold fingers' winter wedding night.

Then let us run
Until the sun's a floating red balloon
To trap in jumping hands
Or follow, dark below the darkest hills,
More hushed than hush of forests, more than still.

(1958)

"GOD THE ALL-TERRIBLE"
(First line of the old Russian national anthem)

Outside the house
The night trembles to enter.
Are we ready to let in
tonight, this night, our guest?

Feel how it presses
close to the outer walls,
hovers at the window's
small-parted mouth.

Must it turn from us, empty?

We need not move
to let inside
the darker dark that shivers separate.
It comes as we desire it.
Do not move.

We have our consummation,
you and I,
each of the other,
But there yet remains
the consummation of the outer night
and our two inner darks.

The one of these three darks I may call God.

No wonder men have gods,
gods or a God, and fear them,
fear Him,
fire-feathered, golden-wild or drumming-black,
or frozen white and candled under boughs of stone.

The night is full of gods,
twitch of black lightnings on the opened sky
shadowing into half-shut rooms
that dare contain
some of the night,
shudder of sleep-spread earth
below the house,
and first in-breathing quivers in the house.
Be still, He comes.

Will He be thunder-dark,
moon-white or rainbow-flowered?
Or will He break us blind?

Close down the picturing eyes,
kiss dumb the worrying mouth,
stroke flat the shaping hands,
touch still the knowing limbs,
and do not wonder whether we shall move
or whether God will breathe.
If He is fear, come rich uncoloured fear,
uncontoured terror:
fear must have an end.

(1958)

WE NEARLY DIED

We nearly died last night.
The dark beat
darker wings,
huge heavy angel wings.
We nearly fell,
full, into lightness of a feather's lash.
We nearly cried
out to where silence sings.

So nearly breathed
no-colour darkness of the underworld
beyond branched fires,
below the hurrying flood,
more dark than caverned water
outrunning water, swift almost to stillness.

Dark as the underside of snow we slept.

But woke and knew
leaves clubbed with snow,
three days' set snow,
and on the snow
stuck pins of frost:
the windows had been armed
with arrows and above the doors hung knives.
The trees wore crowns of thorns.

We were not dead!
You were a bird,
warm, down-headed,
new, down-bodied,
an hour unborn a man.

(1958)

ISLAND

I will tell of a huge sun
Burst like a horn blast
Out of a folded metal sea.
I will tell of a vast unpatterned sky
And of a land so small
It was a ripe round nut that fell
With such a light bell's ring
Into the sea's mailed hand.

(1958)

RESPITE

When midday smoked the snow away
from the paved hill,
steamed the roofs black and bared blue sheets of sky,
stripped to the wind
the city's green outsides,
I dreamed the year less young,
I breathed the time
less stark, foresaw the light less straining.

How very very sweet
suddenly not to matter, not to mean
anything at all,
to lie along the edge of a ploughed field
with scent of stubble after cutting time
on a still day,
no longer frowning through
to where words hesitate or reason hide,
head sunk in whiskery weeds,
back bedded in neglected crumbs of dust,
to lie all day alone
lost as a brown plump pear
denting a small forgotten patch of ground.

So it might be to die,
to brown away to dropping,
formed to roundness, glutted, even flushed,
as one who, giving birth, may breathe past pain:
not bone-sharp, blue-mouthed, mouthing messages
to the dart-eyed hungry live
who have not yet been weaned away from meaning.

Only the young,
the young of all years old,
die, wringing the last drop
of sleepless meaning from the tired air,

for they have lived so terribly awake,
mattered immeasurably,
have signified
with bitter bright intent
and so die staring.

There is no short way out of being young:
the wrinkling years
plough ineffectually,
for every corn-time stands
a pink and pear-pip-breasted child,
purse-mouthed with fixed fierce eyes
to harvest its demands.

One must be young again
many more times,
live spiked and sparking, meaning desperately,
embrace the bitter spring
that dots the days with rebel buds of snow,
bares wide self-conscious grins of light
and grows.

(1958)

PRAYER   (Barra)

Blow high the bubble sun!
Let it be day.
Let a day come,
Seen, not through the haze of myself,
Felt, not through the daze of my own
Frost film of an almost comfortable despair:
Send the day green.

Let a road run
White, not with frost bitten snow, but
Dazzling with ground shells
Round a bright island,
That I within
The thin round bubble shell of day
May walk.
Then let the sun
Fall at the night start with a sleeping body's weight:
That will be all.

(1959)

IN DARK APRIL

In a dark April, angry to be born,
I drum small heels hard on the world's wall home.
Ready to tear
A way out anyhow into soft shining air.

Give to my womb-creased face
The kiss of grass,
Give my new eyes
Touch of warm chestnut leaves
Feeling their first way down.

Those wide blond dandelions
Have not met me before.
They have no memory of another I.
To them my first seen smile.

Born people are quite near
To three-pronged pigeon prints on a sunned square,
And find each leaf and grass a separate green
In a sharp April.

(1959)

FOR SUMMER VISITORS

Leave to me my own soul and wild garden,
the long reach of the sea,
warm stones for me to spread
and to uncrowd my body.

They say there are no pretty coves or inlets.
I say the shingle is a broad shrugged back
uncompromising seas
laugh at or slap, caress or overwhelm.

They say, what do you do here, nothing happens.
I say the sea brims into all my days
and they are full. I say the apples swell
and warm their skins upon the August sun.

Leave me my window wide upon the moon
or closed on paws of snow;
leave me the rain
flung from the mile-off sea, and the salt street:
leave me the sun
slung in the apple trees, sprawled golden rod,
wet snares of shamrock;
leave the saw and squeak
of two tall elms,
the stamp and champ and snap
of cows treading the darkness in the copse
beyond the garden; leave the call of owls.

Leave to me my own heart and wild children,
and do not make them classify their love
with unmeant gratitudes and unfelt smiles:
there will be time enough for them to learn
expedients, when the immediate crop
is stored like apples in a winter room.

Leave them the grown grass and the muddled roots,
frost shapes of fossils, fossil shapes of moss.

Go all your ways and leave me room for stretching.
Leave me the sky,
the sudden dark or the quick flush of sun
outside your categories. Leave me a gate
wide open

Trim your own borders and sum up your sky;
your landscape cut and dry.
Leave me the mist,
a ghost sea running white at my world's end,
and leave me, undefined.

(1968)

BALL IN THE RIVER

Thirteen years strong,
a child's swimsuit stretched to its limits,
eager to swim
where "Swimming beyond here is dangerous",
rain warming the full river,
ready to tread
top branches in sprung wind
till the trees flowed like river weed
and the tide of the mowing field swung close
and caught me off guard.
Brave dreams stretched my venturing body
as the new body stretched my childhood's skin.

From the slackening summer River
Avon I came with a friend,
butterfly clouds brushing the sun
and the water meadows frothing meadowsweet:
sniffing the marzipan scent and spotting
among rose shreds of ragged robin
shell pale marsh orchises,
we ran the river water off our backs,
reached the prickly gravel path, slowed,
passed the sluice gates.
Just a trickle came through.
The top water stood
a stagnant miniature field
greener than grass,
flat with green sequins pushed together.

We had passed it, I said,
going into the full of the sun,
when something caught in the tail of my eye,
hardly seen among pins of light
in my eye and the river.
It could have been

a trick the light was playing,
but I turned,
half bored in drenching heat.

In the too-vivid green, too still
scum, was something round.
A ball?
I was kneeling and could just reach.
I needed both hands.
A strange ball, heavy.
A baby.

A cold fat toddler boy in torn pants.
We stood him, awed.

In no time he was screaming,
but, as though not trusting
such evidence, as though afraid
that any moment he would lapse back
into that cold suspension
in which I'd lifted him,
born, head-first, from the river,
I said to my friend, "What should we do?"
"Try artificial respiration."

So we laid him, howling, down, with his chest in the grass,
and pressed with our brash young hands:
naturally he yelled
more loudly
I picked him up,
his cold softness struggling against me,
his nose running, his screaming close to my ears.
The river whisked out of sight
like a tail flicking off flies.

We walked him round
in our bare feet and our chilling costumes

to a shallow stream where the babies played,
asking, did anyone know him?
At last somebody pointed out his mother.
She had several other children.
She took him, it seemed to us, vaguely.
We explained, more than once, what had happened
on the less frequented stretch of the river,
told of the grass green danger
and the afterthought of our turning,
told of the cold.
But she seemed unimpressed, said, "Oh thank you."

So I relinquished him.
We went to get dressed.
I had a young brother at home, but this one was different.

Would he wander again
with a shifted cat's stubbornness back to the brilliant green
patch into nowhere, this time completely?

When I told the story at school.
admitted regretfully there was no brave deed
needed, I had only to put out my hands
to land him, a fat fish,
admitted, too, that I should have liked to have kept him,
 they laughed, "You, the tomboy.
wanting a baby!"
"I don't want to have one,
I mean, it shall have no father
unless it's the river.
To find one is different."
"Look, she's blushing—even her arms are blushing!"
My giggling could not cover
a kind of quickening.
Through all the river-browned skin of my body
blood glowed, and showed.

I had learned about babies and men
and had not liked what was learned
from the tone of the telling.
That "something beautiful, a flower opening"
could be, in other place or time, "real dirt"
was difficult to know,
and so I chose to ride
the clean green river body
away from being woman.

How could I have known
that, eighteen years after that time,
frost growing at the window
and high tide of snow,
on to the white-towelled bank of my own breast
my hands should take the head
and then the rest
of my real son,
lolled, coolly sleeping
almost too long,
till someone turned,
bringing soft drops of water to begin
the sound of him, the struggling,
and in the stinging winter morning sun
had brought him home,
my own, my river child.

(1968)

CROSS ME A WINDMILL
(Sark)

Pattern a windmill
on a road's rise,
scribble me hedges.

Spike a few poplars,
stretch an oak or two,
carve me no ridges.

Lean my eyes,
lidded with noonlight,
on the land's quiet.
Bend me a river.

No cross of death,
no four-point blunted star,
no cross of iron or wood,
white mountain shrine,
shall beckon me,
but kiss of windmill
on a straight country
that is three-quarters sky.

No-one turns back the earth.
I will not hide for long
in hollow trees
to listen to the grass.

The world breathes on my neck.
Somewhere clouds mass
with poisoned drizzle,
misshapen goats
lumber through dust;
and somewhere else my guilt
in being man

totters on birdlegs
and is child of man,
dragging tall shadows
on his native ground.

Here too was struggle,
smell of death
in cringing hovels,
however the puff-bonnets
jigged at harvest.
Time gone and time to come
throw on this moment
white nets of the spray
that human weather
or the season's wrath
fling up, from hidden seas
to mesh the present
where the still mill
stands, stamped on chaos.

Some places known
and others to be found
are all contained
in this squat tower,
this boat-built landmark
resting between winds.
Though winds and change
erase it in the end,
though ends themselves
erase themselves in all,
give me this day,
cross me a windmill.

(1970)

OF GODS IN GENERAL

We have as many gods as there are people:
some of the noisiest are the smallest ones,
as is to be expected.

When we have finished praying,
or forgetting to pray,
or not intending to pray:

when we have made an interval
in justifying
or not attempting to justify

a day's
or a life's ways;
when we rise from stiffening knees,

and from weeding
out of our time the growth that was unneeded,
what seeds shall we have spared

to unknot
in our sun's
god-fingers?

Deal with your gods as you find fit,
and they will deal with you
as you are fitted.

If you want a god from me
I will take some clear water
and fill a fish bowl,

wait till the water's still,
and say, see, this is my god,
bottled for your inspection.

The population
of gods
runs into millions.

Any one of us can
project a god at will,
the self's outlier.

They come in all colours,
density optional,
likewise significance.

I shall choose to extend myself,
if this is required,
as water, reflecting

anything you may wish to bring,
your face if you choose,
your god if it pleases you.

(1970)

WHEN ALL THE GEENEYED GIRLS

When all the greeneyed girls have got their lovers,
when all young witches' spells blow from their fingers,
when flaxen boys are fathers,
will there be you and me and the long moor,

red-ghosted autumn night and branched horizon,
and some black block, gate can it be or gibbet?
straddling the track into the sweet pine forest?

When loves of friends blushed close at our day's end
we each faced different windows. You and I were
sister and brother even though somehow or other
we had managed to love two children into the winter.

One of them had to be thawed out like poultry
and he is still goose pimpled, while the other
canters off snorting, her mane a whip for our faces.

I could have given you the violet centre,
the violent centre, and left gentler children,
but your loves lived where fairy people thrive,
wisps of the wind and flame half grown or else half human.

I was a mountain myth, a slippery snow girl.
You hunted me on mist of sliding mountains,
but then I was a woman like a woman
with you a blundering boy who did not want to follow.

Through green-starred bogs, on tussock-savage hillsides,
in drizzling larch-hung valleys
and up walled tracks heading the ritual rain
can we walk back the winter?

(1973)

BLACK SHAWL

If I must be old
then take me to a country
where age wears a black shawl,
where the old make shadows
on white still streets
and bending shapes
on slow-coaxed fields
where faces dry like fruit,
hands thickening bark,
go on carrying the wood,

and when at last the old ones
are dug into the landscape
there are some spaces wide enough to see
peopled with bits of sky
and leaf buds,
a wall's corner
and the small winds for goodnights.

(1973)

ZIGGY-ADAM

Ziggy really sang
Screwed-up eyes and screwed-down hair-do
Like some cat from Japan...
He took it all too far...
But, boy, could he play guitar.   David Bowie

Thin long spiky
grower of cacti, worker with wires,
your mind's in squares,
a circuit diagram,
and your heart's battery-charged.
You are all points and angles,
tall as pylons,
a cubist miracle.

Thirteen winters
since you surfaced
out of my slow night
to your snowlit day
with your tall pointed head
and your thrust upper lip.
You were the priceless wax doll no shop sold.

Seven years' wait for you:
I thought that you might sleep for seven years
and I not sleep again.
In nightmares your lolled head
had red-sacked alcoholic's eyes:
you lurched on pavements and the traffic roared.
I could not cross to you.

The next day woke you,
ordinary baby
overnight rounded,
pointed elf child changed for something human.
You were all men,
you were Man,
father and brother
and strange snap-beaked
fastening lover.
Sons were not my kind of luck.

A year and more you milked me. I came human
from your birth's wide desert
and weaned you   with a sister.
Still you were not quite flesh,
the raw bird,
the one feared for,
the feared one.

Spined like a hedgehog
against all intrusion
you have never forgiven
all that is woman.

You take it all "too far":
no halfways for you.
Thwarted, your wraths
can overturn tables.
You gather from anywhere
maps that will take you
all the way everywhere cycleback
down the rain, back
to floorsful of metal parts, gutted old radios,
every scrap sense to you.

Your shoulders hunch your hair into straightness,
burying your neck.
Behind locked doors you scrutinise
your mirror face,
then face us, slot-eyed, from the side. Already
close to your upper lip two faint dark smudges
cannot be washed off.

"Ziggy played guitar..."

(1973)

FOURTH STAGE OF LABOUR (Thirteen years later)

Here is fuchsia, here is lavender.
here the heavy buddleia breathes summer.

I had a wise midwife:
one lifelong winter night she said to me
"Later there will be
a fourth stage. This will have been nothing."

And so it seems
on weed-green evenings
when a strong house moves
with human storming.

You weight is in my eyes.
The waters break
and pains continue
into dry labours.

I would have you again
your few inches of pain
filling the universe.
I would have back the sterilising snow.

I would begin
the labour that must end
and end the labour that had no beginning
and will outlive our lives.

(1973)

CHRISTMAS?

1

Christmas is a wake for the dead, Do we all have to go?
May one or two us bury our year alone
soberly?
The star that stands on the hill
is also a cross
and the church below a tomb
for breaking out of.
Never mind the cake:
All the dark sun is caught
in a shake of raisins,
an orange rounds the earth,
and that means both hands full.

All the thin people
have fingered our rich pudding.

Scrooge had his points.
It is not kindness to be kind at Christmas
because the conscience angel floods your head with light
to beam out of your eyes
and hang limp birds upon your arms,
when, if you choose to scowl in your pinched room,
there's no-one needs be grateful.

2

One Christmas day bells bonged from the cathedral
and tinged from hamlet steeples
in frost-blurred sun, and I was twelve and walking
with my devoutly atheist father
who, prompted by our wartime rabbit dinner,

wished we could go on wandering
dinner-deserted lanes
and nibble bread and cheese in empty pubs.

3

Another Christmas in a midland flat
you and I saw no sense
in sitting out the gasfired end of night,
so swung to sleep
crooked in the hammock of each other's knees,
and rooms below, breaking accustomed quiet,
pounded a party
and the house throbbed into harbour,
all lights but ours awake
while we cut loose from Christmas and were ferried through
the dark.

4

There was that Cairngorm Christmas,
its beer-brown torrents, whispering dusk snows,
miles doubled by snow storms
and nights at noon,
the starting for a mountain with the stars
dripping like baubles, and our noses
needled by pines,
a small forest of deer,
and on the dim Ben side
that day unwrapping like the year's first roses.

5

One Christmas I forget
because soon after,
like a late present battered in the post,
came a first man

to a frightened house.
The first man felt like death inside my life.
Surely no life could grind so many darks
from the clock's humourless face
or slowly skin a day with all its nerves awake
and still emerge with it and you and I
the right side of the snow?

He was delivered packed in silence
like the snow all round the house.
I did not ask whether he was alive
but saw only the moulding of his face
in my one holy moment.
There was no cry.
They listened for a bird's breath
before they wrapped and rested him
and let me sleep like one
who had created earth and heaven.

Adam was Eve's rib.
He was all her parts.
They slept and woke like one.
Snow ringed them in its light.

6

Nine days before a Christmas came her day.
I rode the nightmares of remembered birth,
was sometimes thrown by them.
She thrust with powerful strokes
and yelled her grounding.
They held her up, the shrill blue animal,
stilled to a pagan image.
I called her by a magic Hebridean name,
but soon she fixed us with a straight no-nonsense stare.

That Christmas day we walked a Christmas card,
snow in all the right places,
while she, that woman-of-the-world,
sunk in repletion, her own grandmother,
rounded three generations with content.

7

Christmas is a birth of the light,
the drum of day,
noon and the steaming snow,
the take-it-now,
sugar plum, perfect nut,
wave crook and crown of hills.
You could take your cross
and break it on your knee
or burn it, a Yule log.
Old Omar could come north
to taste the wine of rain
and call for trumpets with no judgement day.
Christmas is a show for the young.
You might as well come.

(1973)

MERRY CHRISTMAS

Stripped from the waist like Lawrence's
labourer flung asleep on a ploughed canvas
he is spread on his bathroom floor,
but no policeman confiscates the scene.

Parents, we drag his drink-logged length
into pyjamas, under blankets,
restore his fourteen-year-old prudery
normally guarded under the bathwater.

In the day's crowing grey,
lowing and braying grey for a nativity,
woken cased in vomit
he is given a birth bath.

We are both sober as a barn wall.

Hoary St. Nicholas,
light him a new year
that does not end in dawn stench,

that needs not turn a body inside out
to find a fire's point on a blade of frost

(1973)

THE LADY'S NOT FOR BURYING

I am not sure I would make
a very good corn god.
I am not worth burying.

I was never much good with a garden.
What the pheasants, rabbits and deer
left uneaten grew bent or stunted, matured
in my absence and toughened.

I'd never feed a village.

You could try me in the sea,
but I am not much better
at staying under water.

I am the sort you burn
and throw in the wind's palm
to cast on a road and stop cars.

Blend me with pebbles
where summer children
bury their parents
in laughing shivery graves.

I will rise, if I rise, in grandchildren.

I will rise, if I rise, in a book,
a shock-headed word-in-the-box
for clever people to argue back my breath.

I will rise, if I rise,
in a village's gossip
to run with the straws
down an ochre street
as the wind wakes.

(1974)

A FAIRY TALE

Summer is where you find it.
It can be a lawn a stride square
and a fenced strip
six feet narrow.

All rainbows grew there
and all scents began there.
All the birds in the district
had made it their headquarters.

There were fairies,
not only at the bottom
but all over it.

The fairies were aunties
draped in scarves the colours of the flowers,
except for the one that was me
in a special fairy outfit
with fairy wings
made by Auntie Rose
in peacock patches of material,

satin and silk from Auntie Amy
who couldn't flit outdoors
like the other fairies
but sat upstairs in her room
in buttoned leggings,
with tiny white doll fingers
weaving her spells
in the shape of blouses
for expensive West End shops.
She could never afford
to make one for herself.
One day, as a very small girl,

her legs had stuck underneath her
before they called it polio.

Auntie Rose took off her fairy
scarf at teatime,
put on a white overall
and let me watch her mixing medicines
at the chemist's shop in the evenings.
I did not learn until I was older
that she sometimes dreamed of poisoning people,
that in her teens she had lost the use of her legs
purely because of her thoughts,
that because she was so bad
she had been psychoanalysed
without having to pay for it.
She was my favourite auntie.

Auntie Em was the strictest.
She was game to be a fairy
but her patience
occasionally ran out.
However, I learned quite early
to be sorry for her as the eldest
Who'd missed all her chances
to be made to work in the house for her mother
and the other eight children.
Plain and scrubbed, her hair in a bun,
she firmly spooned out custard.

Em and Rose were the ugly sisters
of my mother's childhood,
religious as sin,
but to me they were fairy godmothers.

Gran sat on the sofa like a barrel
bolstered with hand-knitted blankets,
hardly able to move an inch

for arthritis, with her hair like dandelion down
and her kind kind face
quite unable to grasp
the martyrdom of her daughters.

Grandad was a small and prickly
gnome, with a voiceful of funny jokes
and a pocketful of pennies.
I didn't know, then, about the time
When he kept them all on £2 a week
and put a Vote Labour bill in the front room window.
How they all cried! Until he took it down.
You can't live in Fairyland and be realistic.

The auntie they called Babe
because she was the youngest
went to work in a office.
She was nice enough
but less magic than the others.
More ordinary, like my mother.

The uncles were all away married,
and Auntie Nob, whose curly head had got her
a name for life, and a husband,

and, of course, my mother
at home with my new baby brother:
she cried to Rose who hugged her.
                              I asked Rose why.
She said "You see your mum's my little sister."
She didn't explain that my dad
was coming home each night as drunk as Christmas.

Rose was the soul or summer,
as far as I knew.
She gave me summers to fly in.
The garden didn't know it was in

the squalid fag-end of a town -
not until all the fairies
had left it one by one.

Grandad was first.
On the chenille-covered table
was a bowl of Cornish anemones
I had brought. I was about eighteen.
I remember writing "anemones
have dogs noses." In the next-door house
the wireless was very loud,
or were we very quiet?
                Gran looked blank
and at intervals would say
"Isn't it time to go and see poor old Dad?
He may want something."

Gran was the next.
              I lived among mountains then
and wrote the aunties a letter.

Released from her duty
of being one point in a triangle
for humping her mother upstairs,
Babe, at forty,
married her boss at the office
two days before I was married,
and took her baby face to the green belt
                where they had
two cats and some rows of peas.

Rose Em and Amy
and their cat – there was always a cat.
There was one called Mike:
when they found it was a she
they went on calling "him" Mike.
Rose would carry "him" round and round the room

78

rocking "him" in her arms,
singing "He'd rather be busy with his little Lizzie,
The girl with the clogs and shawl"
and they all joined in the chorus.

I went with my children to see them.
There wasn't much room for children
between the legs of chairs and the legs of old ladies.
The garden, a faded ribbon,
was ready to put in a drawer.
Most of the magic had leaked away
from the faces of Rose and Em.
I think that Amy was the last
fairy.
                She covered her twisted legs
with a rug and went on smiling,
repeating the last word of everyone's sentence
and dragging it out as though she was not going to lose it...
lose it,
buttering bread and cutting it up
in neat little squares, for the birds.

I forget which year the cat died.

Em died of softening bones.
All her life's hoarded grumbles
were spent upon strange nurses.
Rose's sadness took a year to beat her
down, from the heart outwards.
The cat calendars I sent at Christmas
had one name less each year.

Amy was cheerful
and the birds were cheerful.
Neighbours and sisters called to feed her,
and put her tiny cubes of bread and butter
out on her window sill.

The bread was snapped up.
Most of the food they brought for Amy
they had to eat themselves.
They all said she ate like a bird
(but she was really a fairy.)

Inching across the room full of chairs,
she tripped, and broke her little twig legs
in so many places that plans were being made
for a long-stay hospital.
She stopped eating and drinking.
She was drying up. She was lighter than a bird.
She was a moth.

She has been blown away.

Nieces must sell the chairs.

(1974)

TIDE POOL (Sark)

Out of August red
and through the squint of sunset
come in the sucked-out blue
at the tide's bottom
to cold ledges behind
the postcards of days.
Dare to slide in
where tips of hidden fish
brush the oars of your arms.
Swim calmly to a wall
where white anemones
button the rock,
wait to expand their fringes
at the brim of a new tide.

(1974)

YELLOW POEM

1

Lanes drenched in yellow afternoon
and bridged with thick wall shadows.

The hot bus swinging though them,
branches scraping windows,
girls squealing as a yellow bee circled,

our children's yellow hair
warm on our arms;

house built of blocks of gold
in a village walled with them,

steep meadow of a garden
speckled with yellow clover,

in every gape of hedge a wedge of sea;

noon scattered on the water in new pennies,
brown-gold babies
with eighteen miles of shingle for a rattle,

toddler in a yellow dress,
boy with a yellow ball
to lodge in the sky like a planet,

tree of deep yellow peaches at the garden's top,
above the fence and old field angry with ragwort;

a forest of spurting golden rod
and a skyful of yellow apples.

2

The peach tree died, the yellow apples
have become sparse and small.

The yellow hair has darkened, is obscuring
eyes of a tall son, cheeks of a rounding daughter.

Ten years, The young near middleage, the middleaged
turn old, the old are making spaces.

No quantity of gold could buy us out
of our own selves: each year we had them back.

The yellow house may turn us out one year:
wealth stowed in yellow stone may store an ending.

But days are trumpeted with honeysuckle, nights
are lit with small cream roses,
fresh hay bales mark another year's skyline,
new thatch sits on old houses like a promise.

Summer still comes in with trefoil, yellow flags,
moves on with goatsbeard, dandelions and toadflax:
we still have banks of buttercups invested.

3

Ten further years. In golden poverty
of celandines, that girl
is bedded in the yellow-walled churchyard.

in the fourth spring of her nullity,
fanfared by daffodils.

And we have left to us,
this yellow-lit July,
gold in that man-son's beard,

and in his eyes pin-stars
of wild and gold ideas

that flood his shaken mind
like yellow bedstraw in a summer lane.

So we are rich as heirs to crumbling
sandstone palaces,

or tramps who find fools' gold in a cold ditch.

(1974)

(Part 3 after 1980)

GLYDERS

Go through the rain to winter:
there is the hard route,

rain of crunched slate,
spat scree,
aimed nails,
rain-bite,
hands' white-ache,
eye on the mountains'
rain side
slapped and swelling,
nostrils the cwm's torrent.

On the thrashed ridge are a dozen black Stonehenges
toppled on one another: there a slate-eyed demon
offers you curios not mentioned in the brochures,
bracelets of rain, round bobble-hats to fit
a sodden brain, capes of Welsh wool
for winding up the drowned,

or it's a quartz-lit angel
to wake you from rain-pain
and wink you warm again.

(1974)

AUTUMN SONG

Sky cannot empty out its streaming grief:
lanes choke green with it beyond belief.
Go down rain,
go down without relief.

Sea doesn't know itself from blowing sky:
white along the beaten beach the sea clouds fly.
Go down boats,
go down like a lie.

Anaemic blackberries won't darken, short of light,
speckle the hedges for a bitter bite.
Go down fruit,
go down sour as spite.

What sort of candle will this autumn hold
to others blazing red and bronze and gold?
Go down sun,
go down green with mould.

Other years peel off leaves, flake like tanned skin:
this year snaps green boughs before the browns begin.
Go down trees,
go down and rot like sin.

Most people lose pace, slow bone by bone:
When the race runs off the cliff you don't stop to groan.
Go down life,
go down like a stone.

(1974)

WHAT HAPPENED AFTER THEY
WERE HAPPY EVER AFTER

(or the ballad of the Haunted House)

There was a boy
Who was kind to children.
There was girl
in love with a mountain.

They lit their candles
to tell their stories
and lit their moons
at the tops of alleys.

The back-end season
fell-kids back at school,
first snow on the mountain,
was the time of their wedding.

Seven years later
(not for want of trying)
they built a boy
of bits and pieces

and not long after
they made a girl
of odds and ends.
They were very lucky.

But this man had a mother
and this woman a father
and he had a sister
and she had a brother.

He became his father,
She became her mother
and they blamed each other
like brother and sister.

Their boy hated her,
their girl hated him
and the boy and the girl
they hated each other.

The man dreamed children
in other houses,
the woman mountains
in other places.

The man and the woman
they took their offspring
to the tops of mountains
where the rain was thickest

or the sun was sharpest
or the night was lightest
and they lit their candles
and they fetched their water.

In the wilderness
they were thrown together
but later the children
hated the mountains.

They went their ways
until the woman
returned to the mountains
and then the boy followed.

The girl and her father
stayed home together,
she made him meals
and she told him stories.

The boy led his mother
over the ridges
and she was little
and he was a mountain.

(1975)

FLOUNDERING

They could not fathom each other
though waves were breaking
nor catch each other's drift
though both were speaking.

They wished themselves fishers,
food to be netted,
storms to be cheated
and details of people uncharted.

They wanted ineloquent hands
to be paddles, blank eyes to be lanterns
lighting the wake that their craft
wrote on the page of the ocean.

Too long at sea,
warped and barnacled,
they were lost between shores
like the Flying Dutchman.

(1975)

MOUNTAIN MARRIAGE

No bells rang at that wedding
nor did any holy man
unite them in their plight.

They were rebels
a generation before
rebellion was the fashion.

On the parquet floor
of the Lake District
Registry Office

They stood as agreed
in climbing boots, anoraks
and government surplus

trousers: her one concession
to femaleness long hair
(not then worn by men)

and a green Swedish
stocking cap.
There were two witnesses:

her landlady in best 'at
and the old age pensioner
fetched that morning

from his allotment:
they wouldn't let him
put his collar on.

Her bouquet was a bag
of firm tomatoes
with their green tops on

which smelt delicious.
He took the Woolworth's ring
out of his glasses case:

The Registrar nearly
giggled. But it was no joke.
They meant what they said.

What nobody witnessed
was: his tall father
stiff as any priest

standing up the full
length of his back
and through the top of his head,

which was her cross,
rigidly challenging as any
rockface she had known.

She did not "have to
get married", indeed
there might never be need.

(1975)

HOW WE SPENT GOOD FRIDAY

The runaway horse
put her among the old ladies
and their cut-out triangle mouths
(four death's heads in a row
like an Edward Munch exhibition.)

Outside the ward's
greenhouse heat
was an April afternoon
while this normally shrug-away girl
clung whimpering to my fingers

blind all the afternoon.
Into the greenhouse day
they came with torches
to read her eyes' dark,
wheeled her down passages

to map her brain's bone.
By visiting time,
as the shoes all made a street of it
and a party of talk
with merry rainbow flowers

for the nearly dead,
my child came screaming sick,
a half-day's idiot
hurt into sanity
and into life, awake.

(1976)

NOW

Now it is five hundred million for the loaves and fishes.
Don't be silly said the religious studies teacher
to the girl in a classroom in an over-developed country
who asked what had actually happened,
whether the fishes
had swelled to the size of sharks,
the loaves to a whole bakery,
and why, if he's still alive somewhere doesn't he
do it again with the sharks and the bakeries?

(1976)

Knot my escape ropes,
like sheets to lower me
through night of Prussian blue
in grey moon's company.

Sky-pointing feet may walk
the straight-down neutral crags
abseiling from no-route
to the rope's rags.

Pared to the skull's teeth
of fright may we descend
faced with our lives' cracks
to our time's end.

Peel back the year's snow
to the limbs' brown
and the leaves' loam.
Lie down, down.

(1976)

SOUVENIRS

You came back from Australia wearing a mood stone
to where I had worn the sea stones on my own
with your book of myths and heavy oiled tree shield,
pages of red-tongued flowers to fire my eyes,
the English Channel turning like your stone
in and out of moods from green to black
to violet to blue, then, beast not stone,
convulsing, snaking white along the shore.
A pebble's width between us could have been
the whole earth's still,
                              each single to the bone.

(1976)

SPRING DIRGE

I dream of village greens, I dream a scene
of thatch and whitewashed clouds, horses and children.

I loved this suntanned stone.
Summer comes up like stagelight on it.
I still inhabit

a house of dreams.
Its windows are cross-barred
and teased by spring as each day comes in warmer.

Now claws of bramble claim
my red soil's garden.
I will no longer force a territory
from gentle rabbits.
I leave alone this children's picture book
of tall ears, swollen moon.

In thorn-beaked woods
I look for wet tracks back
to primrose-headed children
who tripped on roots, who are my fallen dreams,
that, having fallen, burn,

burn up the rural roads to towns that bloom
with toxic lights, where frantic music bruises.

Time for a tortoise to unlock its limbs,
unbutton eyes, unglue its winter mouth.
When is your time, my leather-prisoned
son, to shed the hide you carry
into the day's heat? Into your man's age?
How long must I wait here before which season
your mouth may be prised open?

(1977)

PARTY

Five gallons of scrumpy cider from the farm
in a plastic supermarket skin
hauled like a smugglers' barrel to the beach
by the underage drinkers
at the end of a summer
at the end of a road
at the end of a day
dripping into the sea,
the red fruit slipping
into greenbottle water
the slow waves heaving,
breathing with excitement
as the denim drinkers
clamber up the shingle,
girls with inkblue eyelids,
boys alight with badges,
dragging their booty
into the fishing hut:
hold your breath parents
awake in the village
as the wide-eyed hours
dilate into the morning
and the clattering and shuffling,
the sniggering and stumbling,
the lingering and the fumbling
begin in the square.

(1977)

FAIT ACCLOMPLI (Mother to a seventies teenager)

Graphics by Roger Dean on Genesis' record sleeves.

I cannot rewrite you like a poem:
you are published for all to see.

I cannot edit you, a film:
you have gone out live.

I cannot prune you, your prickles
of science fiction size.

I cannot tame you, no cub:
all's left is to take cover,

or meet you where the roots
claw skies and pose as trees,
you rag-winged monster-bird.

(1977)

COUNSELLOR

Bountiful lady,
serve me your ear upon a coffee saucer.
I am the talking poor.
Sharp as a set alarm my tread rings out
on the brown polished lino stairs to where
you hold your roof-top court,
and what I ask of you I am not sure.

I bring you my despairs
in shopping bags.
Your eyes are lent me like a library book.
The middle of my week
is focussed on your frown of sympathy.
I carry down the street
my charity orange, your last phrase or look.

You wait for me to speak,
giving me sanctuary
from my mistakes, misfortunes, or the far down
long grave of the beach.
Your mouth relaxes to acceptances.
My four unfinished lives
I unwrap, pain by pain, to the sore skin.

Lady of last resorts,
when you get up to leave
your filed confessional, turn off the heat,
button your coat,
do the inept, confused, uneasy, buzz
in your head still, or, cleared by your concern,
at the street door who is it that you meet?

(1977)

GARDEN

It is a different country
at the entry
of the night,
it is a white
sky from which the elms
have been extracted,

there is the unexpected
bite in the June air
and that pared
thumbnail moon,
grass deep enough to drown
and bramble snares,
bats like black butterflies,
the itching rain of midges,
high black hedges
in cut-out individual leaves,
wild roses like small lights,

the foaming elder wave
licking the house that floats
down in its cave of trees,
a small housewreck,
but through and over all
and out of cracks
of buildings, into nostrils
the sweet breath
of honeysuckle trickles.

(1978)

HOUSE PLANT

If a cactus could look at its peculiar
feelers
it might feel as I do seeing you,
saying, what have I grown in my house to trail
weird tentacles in front of my face,
off shoots for your display
of my most secret nature?

All that you were to become
has gone through my hands
and out of my hands,
a strange long extra finger.

How does a cactus draw its nourishment
from a few dusty inches of stale soil
and all the months without water

to push out in July three pure red flowers?

(1978)

THE MARRIAGE BED

Twenty-five years wed
they tired of sailing to sleep
or storming awake
in their spine-curling hammock
slack with resentments, rare erratic passions,
so they ordered a new bed
firm and back-bracing
to rest them for the rigours of their middle years.

Men struggled up the stairs
with the mattress, weighty with all that extra
percentage of steel.
Luckily the base folded
in half. It was a bed wide
enough for most differences of opinion.

The new and the old one
filled the room, apart from the laid-out apples,
boxes of surplus books and more spare bedding.
To the new they must get accustomed,
like sleeping on the floor, no sinking in.
The old was a wonderful trampoline.

There were now no jumping children
but slumped teenagers preferring
to spend their nights on other people's floors.
The Social Services sent for,
a small man with a much too small van called.
The neighbours, seeing him staggering

into the street with mattresses thought they were moving.
"I can't take that bed" he said, it's unyielding metal
making the hall a cage. Just then the dustman
(palm crossed with silver) hoisted it above him,
fed it into his grey van's masticating jaws
that crunched it up, leaving only the smell of refuse.

(1978)

AQUARIAN

You were a child of love but love that could crumble,
soft chalk cliffs that humans should not attempt, only
                                                    seagulls
touch with the utmost delicacy.
Was it not in my power to reach you, you father's to
                                                    reach me?
Can the man who began you not find you?

Once in my dream we were swimming, three people together,
in an estuary heavy with ropes of kelp, umbilical,
the open sea a light-line getting no nearer,
your head going under,
I losing your hair in the long weed.

Here in the daylight your streaming hair flashes round
                                                    corners,
tugs you away, and back, later on, in the roadlights.
Now in a chair with your shivering hands and your voice
                                                    under water
you mirror the child that my childhood pulled out of
                                                    the river,
like an omen, not of your flesh but your wavering spirit.

(1978)

THE TIED HOUSE

Black lace tree patterns on white evening water,
the yellow eyes of houses opening,
and home to no home I am carried.

I have worn that house like a dress,
it is being slipped off me.
I am undressed,
          unhoused,
                deposed,

no queen of my castle
nor ghost of my ruin.

In the time of the cuckoo,
the daylight blue,
lilac to breathe
and the slopes green as freedom,
unpacked and unshielded
I have to get into
the house of my difference,
the neutral place,
          a homeless
                space.

We shall rise like actors
acting beginnings, uncostumed,
we shall stretch out to,
and test, our elements weight

and we may be light
as twigs on the water or
heavy as sandbags,
standing an effort
like pushing a rock uphill,
like breaking out of
a life, or breaking into
                              a living.

(1979)

ON THE JETTY

This could be a steamer travelling to elsewhere,
Travelling the brown iron sea away from here,
The seafront houses washed in evening sepia,
Little trees of seaweed waving their drowned hair,

And I could be a traveller moving out of nowhere,
Moving with the deck slats from a dead-wood town,
Quay shrinking, swallowing the tiny heads of pin-people,
Moon's head surfacing, a very tired old clown.

This could be the wake of my craft in the channel.
Clean lane of moonlight apart from the shore.
That could be the line at the end of my planet,
Cancelling all the going that has gone before.

(1979)

ADAM IN AUTUMN

Sad son, gold-bearded god of the dark boundaries,
what is there left to give you on this night of roads?
What may I send you on this wind of leaves
to light the drop
into your deep mind-shafts?

This is a crown
of crisp leaves for your temples:
my prince, I give you
a golden necklet
of lamps along the motorway.

From my hands come
the gilded windows lit in the tall towns
I pass through and would pass with you this night,
brooches of cat's eyes and rich rings of rain.

Claim your inheritance,
defend your opulence,
a harvest moon your shield,
O my gold child.

(1979)

DETERRENT

Little puckered mother
who held your child for
nine branding hours while
her life peeled off her,
kneeling to the water
to float her a pink candle
thirty five years later:

river of paper
coloured lanterns
silently moving
through Hiroshima
their yellow tear-flames.

A telephone only
was held to my face
the hours my daughter
was not surviving
the blaze in that place
she offered her loving,
lit from her life by
hands she was serving.

The coroner
advised her father
--she is in there: when your enter
it is better if you do not lift the red
sheet.
      When I asked him if he had
he shook his head and I said—No-one
must see her, not her brother
or her god either,
no-one at all,
my face a waterfall,
friends coming and going,

tip-toeing:
we should have howled
down heaven together.

Small shaken mother,
if I could bring
my hand to yours
an interpreter could
explain, I come from a nation
prepared to burn children.

(1980)

AFTER THE (Mission Hostel) PARTY

Ten women residents with no warning sign:
One choked upon the smoke, then there were nine.

Nine women residents in a hazy state:
Flames beat back one of them, then there were eight.

Eight women residents looking up to Heaven:
Jesus came down for one and then there were seven.

Seven women residents, cats on hot bricks:
No fire alarms to sound, so then there were six.

Six women residents, just about alive,
Found no extinguishers, so then there were five.

Five women residents making for the door:
One saw the mouth of hell and then there were four.

Four women residents, down on bended knee:
One made her peace with God and then there were three.

Three women residents, nothing they could do:
One jumped from a window, then there were two.

Two women residents, one who had begun
To work for the others, stopped, then there was one.

One teenage co-worker, holy as a nun,
Stayed in her holy sleep, and then there were none.

(1981)

At the head
of the cross
is the face
of a god.

At the intersection
of the cross
is the heart
of a man.

On the trunk
of the cross
is the blood
of a beast.

On the arms
of the cross
are the hands
of a child.

At the foot
of the cross
is the head
of a woman.

(1981)

I SPENT AN EVENING

I spent an evening with life my lover
and music my deliverer.

Life turned the white walls golden
as a morning colours mist.

Outside the winter
hissed in blowing leaves

but in the shelter
of its glowing shell
my room was singing.

Life sang, light hung,
and if the rest is weeping
and when creeping colder thieves

this time and music
and the quick of being lived,

my song will say:

one day I spent an evening
sung to delivery
by life the loving.

(1981)

LEAVE ME WITH TREES (after Iceland)

To travel, on buses like boats riding waves of mud and lava,
on shaggy-head horses, our feet nearly touching the ground,
in planes frail as insects, the pilot handling our luggage,
or, in our own boots, brittle rock, gritted ice,
slit snow, the valleys cobbled with boulders,
waterfalls drowning our voices, our eyes rounding
as the blue balloon of the geyser pops, spurting its steam,
and lead-blue beachless shores unroll like ocean shallows,
or we bump, hump after hump, through the day-long
grey cinder tundra of the interior,
or in the Esso, Coca-Cola village,
the flaxen children line up to be photographed:

this is one picture. Holidays have some hours
of blue, white, gold, in a month of drizzling summer.
But, to live there? In a corrugated iron and concrete town
of fish-wet wind slapping the flat house faces,
the long planed Viking cheeks
and jaws jutted against the climate, cagey
of thawing face to face as the spring mountains,
the houses over-hot, sealing themselves
against the threatening, always imminent, wild?
To treasure inch-high trees,
teach the head's top to emerge without protection
as though the skull is open to the thin glass air
with white night daylight entering the brain's cracks
through widening eyes, as though the eyes are lidless?

Then the dark, weeks of dark:
this we have not experienced, nor short summers
of scouring suns, their brilliance not quite sane:
I tell you it is settling halfway to the moon,
and only people born not quite in time
take root in this razed soil
defenceless to the wind's pull,

116

no clay, no settled stone, no breathing forests,
the land's crust crumb-like, shifting,
mountains whose heads catch fire,
rivers that swell out of control
and the cold edge of air abrasive as lava scree.

I was no patriot, snivelling of English Aprils,
but now that I am back under the reassurance
of trees, enfolding of trees, enclosing and bending over,
neck-stretching of trees, I feel this surprising dependence
on trees, this resistance to exposure
on a land not merely nude but skinned and scraped.

When we first talked of moving to Iceland I had not lived
a month without trees, or with only toys of trees,
I had not lost a summer or stayed with houses,
toys of houses without stone or brick, slate, thatch,
used sharp air like a drug, then wanted to resist it,
so I say, leave me with old stone a winter longer,
leave me with trees at least another summer.

(1981)

ICELANDIC HIDDEN PEOPLE WELCOME
A LONE IMMIGRANT

Grey is the quay and empty.
Grey are we and lumpy.
Translate us as fairies,
elves, we are definitely
not the English garden variety.

There will be no friends waiting.
They are probably busy
getting themselves ready
to leave their bodies
under their sheep-coloured bedclothes,

and fly into the night
where their white friends wait
until grey daylight
that will soon be short
as a midday snack.   Each spirit

hails you as one of us,
rare as winter grass,
precious as three-inch trees,
with your own brightest personal
aurora borealis.

(1983)

ANTIPODES

Standing the season on its head, he said:
I'll take you to summer,
I'll give you a rock as red
as a burning wall.

Last year we left our spring
for the Finnish snow
and a river ten feet thick;
this winter we will go
desert journeying.

I'll fly you over ice
for hours and hours and hours
and through three fiery sunsets in reverse:
I'll take you to a land of fiery flowers.
Woman, you could do worse
than travel by my side.

The desert's wide.
Life may not be complete,
but I will walk you through a dream of heat;

and when it rains
it's rain you've never seen:
the Rock turns blue;
the tourist jeeps have trouble getting through
for rivers everywhere,
and little black kids with their ginger hair
swim in the roads.

In Alice Springs a homesick waitress says:
"Remember me to England in the spring—
it is the crocuses..."

(Under the crocuses our daughter lies,
under their white stems with her worm-white eyes.)

(1983)

NEW YEAR INTENSIVE ENCOUNTER GROUP

They removed our watches, but could not wipe out daylight,
sunset or human rhythms, Timepieces proved dispensable.

Some of us were given time, some tried to snatch it,
some were told they had taken too much.

Time which could not be disposed of, was slowly squandered
in daylight discos, wordless follow-the-leader
and a few verbal lynchings.

That boat we, chain-gang, rowed
in time with barked commands
had never yet seen water.
"Harder ! Faster! Urged the bank of lady (bigger than a boathouse)
"til you go bananas! Row! It's the irrational we're after."

Those tears we cried while sitting eye to eye
were assessed grimly, found inadequate
by a humourless, goose-stepping boy, his eyes bullets,
pitch of the voice "Adolf's" (he known, harmlessly, as Fred.)

Line them up, women versus the men, men v. the women:
"Tell them what you think of them! More volume!"
(Before today most of them hadn't met.)
"Wimp!" shrills, the pale girl to her instant partner.
He wilts. " You feeble little wimp!" she dares, him.
His hackles rise like antlers:
it takes six men to hold him down.
The women scatter, whimpering

Now it is insult-your-parents time, so take it out on mummy,
and if it seems to you that mothers seldom (your own and you
included)
actually intend their children ill, you are a double target.

"Yes all stand in a ring and scream at her! (witch-baiting)
"No, she musn't answer back."

Two women shared a room.
One didn't want to be born, the other didn't want to die.
One closed the window against the breathing night and the world's
                                                              sounds.
The other opened it, let in world, wind and a clock's chiming.
One pulled the blind down, not wanting to find out the hour's light.
The other compromised, left it, tried to lie dead, waiting to rise
                                                              again,
hours awake in the dark, peering for tomorrow through shutters,
and up at first greylight, closing the window for the womb-fast other.

The unborn one, riven with screaming, headed
for the bosom of the wide womb-queen in the next room,
shrieked "Hell and damnation! That woman with fingers
like black twigs will rip me out of the dark – oh bury me
or I will burn her. She is stained with pain,
infested with death" (as life is) " Oh save me from being!"

Even so, the year entered, bawling, a bearded baby,
sobbing, a little girl with grey hair, trembling, a child in jackboots.
The night-air-fiend who was the bad witch-mother
left half an hour before the year had come and would not join the
                                                              party.
They gave her back keys, cash, but forgot her watch.
It did not matter. She had time on her side
in a night wide as a moment or a lifetime.

(1984)

122

THE FARMYARD SET

Here's your farmyard set.
The cows are painted
Black and white:
Just what you wanted,

Brown shiny hens,
Beige lumpy sheep,
White toothy fence,
All for you to keep.

Green stick-up trees,
Fit-together hedges:
That should give me peace,
Keep you quiet for ages.

Plastic horses
And a donkey,
Clip-clop noises:
Did you thank me?

Here's your little hill.
It's bright and wooden:
If it was real
It would get too sodden.

Here's a month of rain
Falling on the ground
You can just wipe clean
With hardly any sound.

Here's your pretty house
Made out of a kit.
When the west wind blows
It shakes a little bit.

Here's your brand new bike
Standing in the hall.
Ride it if you like-
Mind you don't fall.

Here's your fluffy cat
(Don't forget to feed it)
Cuddly, warm and that.
You don't know when you'll need it.

Here's a daughter for you.
She's done in oils
With a jacket of blue
In a frame like the royals.

No, she's not coming back.
She lives in the sky
That's just round the back
And ever so high.

Here's your dear old hubby,
Nice and kind
With his chin all stubbly
And his clever mind.

Why don't you play
With your farmyard set?
You can stay in all day,
Then you won't get wet.

You can turn up the heat,
Then you won't be cold,
Have all you want to eat.
You should be good as gold.

You're a lot better off
Than most people are,
With all this good stuff
And rides in my car.

Did you mention love?
There's love for me:
The love I have
Lives across the sea.

What did you say?
That isn't fair?
My love's away
Through hours of air.

That's one small thing,
Just now and then,
My girlfriend, young.
Well, you know men.

Into her bed
I'll sometimes go.
If you'd not said
You wouldn't know.

If you'd not been prying
Or if I'd lied
We could still be lying
Side by side.

If you hadn't made
Your discovery yet,
Then you would have played
With your farmyard set.

(1986)

ANOTHER BLOODY SUNSET?

From everywhere you went you sent me sunsets,
postcards of days' ends, calendars of cancelled years,
from Colorado purple to Brazilian scarlet,
Mexican ochre, cloudberry gold from Norway,
deep pink of the wild coastal roses of Denmark,
Japanese cherry-petal blush, orange of Chinese roses,
pale orchid pinks and mauves of Swiss May pastures
and garish flaring of New England fall:
reds menstrual and placental, reds burning.

They were not planned as wounds. You thought it friendly
sharing these tearing colours, though you could have known
I have my own sunsets, staining the willow stems
vivid with your absence, clouds slashed with as much gore
as anyone could wish. Is a hearth friendly
that leaves its glowing guests turned into ash?

The low sun's blaze comes to announce its darkness.
I should have read your sunsets years before
you finally dragged the day's face down my sky,
buried it for me in a round black hill,
then took your red hands to light up her hands
and sent me sunsets:

        "Sunset in Siberia,
grainy, maroon, your message (from the train) "Siberia
is a wonderful place." Imagine Siberia
extending in front of your window, and you with your biro
dashing off postcards.

Your Christmas, Nepal,
brought me a *set* of postcards: "Mount Qomalangma,"
fist of cerise snow against glossy tourist crimson
to stand beside my wrinkled holly-berry sun
in the bleeding to its death of this kind season,
in the setting of my year behind your burial mound of
fictions.

(1987)

TRAVEL

Road, long as a scream.
Drove you out of my dream.

Rails, sharp as stormlight,
Cut you out of my sight.

Wings, hard as the ground,
Moaned you away, out of sound.

Sea, shoreless as space,
Dragged your face from my face.

Woman, young as a leaf,
Wooed you into my grief.

You, old as a tree,
Pulled roots, tore them from me.

However far you move
I have harboured you in my love.

(1987)

A DREAM OF LEAVES

Jangled from too many dreams of vanishing buses,
of seeing trains pulling out, of forgetting my luggage,
I fell into a dream where you and I lived in a circle
of houses around a green (each the home of a friend)
and I asked you, stretching my neck to look up at the trees,
at their leaves fully grown, vivid heart-shapes of lime
and the darker long splayed hands of horse-chestnut,
"What's the date? June? May? April?" (You didn't answer)
staring in unbelief, breathing the air of leaves,
until my open window's unseasonably
mild January breeze breathed me awake.

I stood up, walked, still deeply, slowly breathing,
my limbs easy, my head filled up with leaves
like a tree's top.

          Now, tight white knots in cotton,
bud catkins dot the willow shoots. A stencilled
moon, half disc cut out of cloud, stuck on the blue
page of the day, is part of a collage
deceptively benign.

          I may have years alone
with no more dreams filling my head with leaves,
breathing me ease,

          will have no more of you
than photographs of our shared summers and the black
naked sticks of our written winter words.

(1988)

BECAUSE I DO

Because I do, I don't end letters "Love."
He writes "love" lightly, living with another.
He writes to me as sister, aunt or mother:
His kindness is the kind that sponsors give.
Because you are, I don't start letters "Dear."
Though I am not, you do, and send me gifts,
As though to hide confirmed and final rifts
With these rich blooms, to make the gaps appear
Narrowed by petals, gently closed by leaves -
A forest in a basket, ivy, palm,
African violet for your past home:
Your presents are the kind a lover gives,

So I will keep them, love them, send you word
To thank you. They are what you can afford.

(1989)

POSTCARD FROM DENMARK

A carnival of sails, triangles, blue, green, red,
strung out like pennants in the ink-blue harbour,
the rigging, black spires downturned on flat night
water, with the points of harbour buildings,
still water blotted with white lights, that festive
bunting of bright boats, the sky another
harbour, ultramarine, and, farther off, a bracelet
of lights, lengthened to lanterns at the harbour's corner.

Partner of thirty years, what does this picture
celebrate? The dark blue water of recall
brings me the beached boats of a holiday,
line-tracks in pale sand, ropes, and the coloured
sails, the miles we walked, the powdery high dunes,
the long strands' cool hard edges where we ran
naked into the waves' glitter, as is normal
in that country.

       Only by puzzled stages
I came to know we had not really travelled
together.

       Still unaware, one evening I set out
alone (you not in the mood) along the shore.
The weather turned, wind running from the sea,
cold rain coming with darkness and distortion
of time and distance making every exit
from beach to road alike. Sodden in summer clothing
and flapping sandals, stupidly I called
at the one lit house, the wrong one. Finally
a further light eyed me through trees. Arrived,
dripping, I found you anxious. Did you think
I might have drowned?

These days you often take
your younger wife, your son the age of our
grandson, to this coast, and, this latest trip, you send
these happy flags to me. Do they commemorate
a hollow anniversary, as street parties
dance for a war?

It is as though I have
no valid passport to the land you claim.

(1994)

ÖRAEFAJÖKULL – THE CLIMB

I collect highests: I had ticked off Nevis,
Snowdon, Scafell Pike, Carrauntoohil in Ireland,
Austria's Gross-Glockner, Sweden's Kebnekaise,
Norway's Glittertind, Galdhöpiggen,
(either, top peak, if crowned with enough snow.)
Iceland's remained to be added to my list.

First, the typical cinder-scree, hours of it,
all of the others Icelanders, tall, male,
except for the two girls, twenty-one and in training,
the three of us at the back, but moving steadily,
stamp, slide, stamp, steepening, theoretical summer
established only by the snowline's level,
at which we roped, two ropes, ten on each of them,
a guide at back and front, I somewhere in the middle,
damp chill penetrating through all my layers.

While we prepared for snow, one of the leaders
said, without ceremony or apology,
"How old are you?" I said "Wrong side of fifty."
"How wrong?" "Five years wrong." (He'd said in the office
where I d' booked the trip, "Do you think you are capable?"
And I 'd replied, " I've done Snaefellsjokull"...
"That's not the same."...) This snow, soft, slippery
as skyr, was knee-deep. Between every footstep
of the man in front, I had to make an extra
leg-step. Some of it was thigh-deep. Troll-beard mist-strands
woven with ice-dew brushed us, while my ice-axe
developed a will of its own and fought with the rope-loop
because my hands were ghost hands. After forever
of up, in, up, and an age of panting
while I tried to repeat, for a timeless stretch, the controlled
panting at the moment of giving birth,
I ventured, "Would it be possible to slow?"

The man in front said " I will pull, you up -
just let me..." I said "No"- puff - "Let me climb-
please- just a pause." Said he of the age-question,
from the other rope, "If you are too exhausted
one of the guides will have to go back with you."
"It's the pace, my short legs. I could make it if
you'd let me off the rope. I can't get lost.
I' ll go up in the footprints." "No, that is not safe."
The rest stood frowning in the chewing cold,
arrested by our argument, until,
with a flash of lateral thought, one of the guides
speechlessly chopped a length off the end of the rope,
and tied me on, motioned the rest to continue,
then me to follow him. He adjusted his pace
to mine. In the language of rhythm we ascended
in the others' steps, with the others out of sight,
on stairs of cloud, wrapped in a sheep-white dream,
sky and ground one off-white. After- how long?-
we reached the plateau and the coloured shapes,
and talking. There we stopped. He took some snuff,
turned, offered me some! Smiling, I declined,
our breath clouding through clouds. This was as high
as any of us would go, beyond, "too dangerous -
dense fog, crevasses."

                    Returned to a main rope,
I faced a further fall from dignity
as my group charged, beating the snow to foam,
and dragging me, spreadeagled, down the slopes.
Much later, off the rope and out of cloud,
we jerked down lava scree that doesn't run
and I was level with the girls again.

In the late evening, ending our twelve hours
up on the mountain, near the valley floor
four small, bright-sweatered children greeted us
with handfuls of the tiny pink star-flowers

134

and offered two or three to each of us.
My stone legs lightened, ran: we, mountaineers,
were garlanded, bouqueted, by play-school kids,
unworthily in my case, the unease
of chopped rope's end tickling my conscience, but
I seemed forgiven by the Utivists
if not the mountain's top, invisible
as Viking ghosts or elves or thunder-god,
or thousand-years-new God the merciful
that sits as lightly as a Lopi woolly hat
planted upon a pagan mountain's head.

(1997)

TABOOS

I've never eaten person.
In the past I did
Eat sheep, cow, pig, hen,

But, at fifteen,
I didn't fancy any
Things that ran or hid

Or looked at me with eyes
And opened a pink mouth,
That squawked, squealed, bled,

Moaned loud in labour,
Called across a field
To its wobbly new-borns.

But when my children,
Embarrassed in a village
As the sole vegetarians,

Asked me for bacon,
Beef, lamb chicken,
I did, for a time, weaken,

Complied, now and then,
Only to make them seem
Of their tribe, not alien.

Beside the crashed plane
In the Andes, survivors
Agonised, food gone,

On making their first cut
Into their dead friends
To remain alive.

But the meat barons
Had no compunction
Feeding herbivore cattle

To their own species
In the sacred cause
Of profits: no taboo.

Some people died too.

Well, maybe it's better to eat
People already dead
To save some stranded lives

Than to kill and consume
Live creatures with human
Parallel parts—leg, shoulder, bum—

When there are so many
Ready alternatives.

(1998)

VALENTINE SONNET

I chose no love instead of dilute love.
I chose the mist, the snowdrops wide and browning.
I watch the bobbing harbour from above:
I don't embark, so I will not be drowning.
I wake each day to my own wordy head.
I gave you to her like a toy white rabbit
Its parent-child no longer takes to bed,
Revert to my old solitary habit
Learned through the decades while I seemed with you,
Greet early red camellias on my wall.
I dream alone while once I dreamed with you,
Value this space, donated by you, all.

        I must have lacked the lessons that she knew:
        I had no other teacher, friend, but you.

(1998)

THE LONG CLIMB (Following a stroke)

1. Waking

The ground is too low.
The air is too high.
I am suspended between.
A short road is too long.

But in early spring
in the early day
with the first cup of tea
and the bedside lamp
and black rooks circling
in the dark blue window of sky

like words, like hopes,

before the aches
and efforts begin
before the buttons
and dishes and taps,
before the staggers
and stiffenings,
before the weight of limbs

I am my rested mind.
I am made of air,
down-light.

I live for this hour.

In my room corner
stand my mountain boots
and Swiss walking pole.

I keep in myself
glaciers, deserts,
forests, horizons,
buffeting oceans,
and audience for my words.

As the sky pales
bringing floors, walls,
windows, of sunlight and trees
like journeys on T.V.

I prepare my damaged person
for its close limits.

By my back door
snowdrops mass,
ivy is outlined in frost
and first violets
are sugared flowers
on a festive cake.

But as the day dims
drags down my choices
and I hope for sleep
to drown me kindly

I am already
impatient for morning,
the dark blue spaces
and the whirling wings.

2. The Edge of Summer

Day after day it was fine.
I cannot remember
such a springful of light.

Every morning
was blue and filled
with glittering birds.

Trees were lit
with green brilliance.

Even rain, which was rare,
seemed to sharpen birdsong.

There was no-one to share
such a spring. To my friends
spring was like this. It was nothing
out of the ordinary.

I came home to the news
that the foot and mouth virus
was closing the foot paths
as the stroke had
the paths to my brain.

Far fells were out of bounds
as were the near small hills.

Two months before the blow
I was descending
from the top of a mountain
to the valley evening.

Now the slope
to road from my front door
presents a challenge.

But the wild came to my door,
Forget-me-nots, primroses, scented violets
with cowslips, bluebells, crab-apple blossom,
kingcups in silted pond
a garden path's hike away.

I do not own my body: my brain does
That is the seat
of all uselessness
and all possibilities.

It has left me
sight, thought and breathing,
spring, and the edge of summer,
green, and the day of colours.

3. Rose

Coastal mist
cools the day.
There is no point in saying
I suffer, I am less than myself
when this scarlet velvet
rose has opened
into the grey-white
reduction of daylight.

Yesterday's and
tomorrow's sunlight,
today's rose scent
must carry me.

Hawthorn browns,
elder creams,
lilac bows with its weight;
honeysuckle and late
apple still blossom.

Evening pearls,
thins sea fog.
Sea is a mile distant,
as a gull flies
over rutted fields,
across a lagoon
of swimming birds,
down the steeply
piled pebbles.

On still nights after gales
I hear waves roll and fall:
sea is a mile distant,
far, so far.

4. Chapel Hill, Abbotsbury

It was a day too blue to forget.

With my hospital stick
I inched upwards
on the year's longest day.

You cannot be a pessimist
and walk uphill.
When eyes lift

and feet follow
mountains of hope rise with you,
no peak is too small.

This is the top I dreamed
When I climbed in mind
without a body.

It is the crest of my wishes,
the tiny southern hills
alpine in triumph.

The chapel, sun-gilt crown,
began my former walks,
but stands, my goal, today.

The mile-off band of ocean
I swam in, forty seasons,
lies for my eyes only.

The first step of a stile
enthrones me
as I breathe summer.

The lane below is pungent
with vetch, mallow, comfrey,
knapweed, campions, sorrel,

their warm dry essence
remembered, and returned into the now.

(2001)

MY JURASSIC COAST

One wind-rocked day, third of a century
ago, we took our infant-school-age children
to Charmouth, much too early in the season,
the sea too wild and dangerous for swimming.

We gathered fossils, as we might pick flowers,
scoop windfall apples, as we had no tool.
Out of the cliffs we heard a hammer ring.

We picked up time-carved samples we found left
among the beach stones, all the delicate
etchings of plant or shell or animal
and a half-ammonite; saw to our surprise,
giant pebble shapes of soft clay. We could print
our hands upon their surface. Would they stay,
that day's engravings, when the rocks grew hard
for children of far future time to find?

Our children's bucket, filled with fossils, went
to school, their village school their father ran,
closed just a decade later. Then the small
museum that contained the fossils moved,
along with log book with the copperplate
records of past teachers, secret lives
of all the village childhoods dating back
for generations, prizes, punishments,
parasites, truancies, and the blocked drains,
to the next school to house the dwindling young.

That fossil day's young boy, now middle-aged,
lives far from here, his younger sister's bones
below a name-carved stone. Their father lives
a different life with his new family now,
and on my brain, the still undamaged part,
like fossil prints on rock, that distant day
is pictured, in my minute scale of years.

(2004)

SPRING SONNET

I used to travel far and high and deep,
Distance, profundity and altitudes
But now I travel only in my sleep
And on the highs and fallings of my moods.
I dream long ridges, rearing cliffs and seas
That I will swim towards the setting sun.
I stand above steep shingle, sliding screes
I am about to leap upon and run.
Stiffly I wake with locked legs, weighted feet
That must be coaxed into obedience.
My life must focus on the near, and greet
The present with its altered circumstance.

Spring bracken stands like lost time tightly coiled.
Each curl of every bluebell holds a world.

(2005)

07 - The poem to end poems (but it won't)

Seven's magic number. On the night
After the year had dawned, I had this dream:
I'm on a poetry course. Try as I might
I cannot write a thing. I have no theme.
Others are busy writing. If I come
Into the group or wander off alone
My page stays empty and my pencil dumb.
Waking, I hunt for words that I may hone
Down to a statement anyone has not
Already heard repeated to the death
And one which does not mean, again, "So what?"
But gives the year new truth for its first breath.

War kills, poverty starves, the sun destroys
The life it gave... Fade out the poet's voice...

(2007)

WALLS

There is a wall between me and the sea.
While, in the dream, I swam from the wall's gap,
the woken shore ran walless for long miles.
Awake, I cannot swim, myself the wall.

I used to run in from the steep bank, swim
far out on the gold track of the late sun,
but now the mile that walls me from the waves
can seem a hundred, over flooded fields.
The sun drowns in my window, and is gone.

There is a wall between me and the sun.
Slow stick-supported walking does not warm
as my strong striding did in the past frosts.
Later a too-hot sun will run me down.

Years pile and fall that wall me from my love.
We send each other friendship from afar.
The walls of distance build around our son
and walls of churchyard soil enclose our girl.

There is a wall between me and my life.
Remembered life suffices. This I learn,
and keep a wall of pictures to recall
seas, hills and suns, two children and a mate,
and self as strong as rocks, waves and the world,
outwitting walls and free as today's gale.

(2007)

VILLANELLE: PAIN NOT POETRY

Pain is not poetry. Pain is basic prose
In black and white without an ornate word.
Pain is the plainest speech that language knows.

The story has no end. It does not close.
The music does not calm with what is heard.
Pain is not poetry. Pain is basic prose.

Our final pain stays with us, only grows.
And finds no exit, cannot be deferred,
Pain is the plainest speech that language knows.

The law forbids we terminate its throes.
The pain-gripped human shouts "This is absurd!"
Pain is not poetry. Pain is basic prose.

It rushes into sleep and nightly goes
On, on and on, as though the darkness stirred.
Pain is the plainest speech that language knows.

Days start like breaking glass. I may suppose
That proof of life is what can be inferred.
Pain is not poetry. Pain is basic prose.
Pain is the plainest speech that language knows.

(2009)

WITCH TO ANDERSEN'S MERMAID

The Sea Witch said to the girl
who was limping along the shore
with a drawn and aged face
'You were once a fantasy
invented for children's minds.
You even learned to swim
into a prince's dream.
In asking to be human
you chose reality,
infirmity, and a death
that lasts for many years.

'My powers are limited
when I deal with human things.
Had you stayed a maid of the sea
I could have given you
hundreds of human lives
alive in the human brains
of the ones who still repeat
old stories to their young.

'Your youth was spent in the sea,
the home of the flickering fish
 and the ribboning weed.
The blue-green window waves
that sunset and sunrise
tinted with gold ans rose
once framed the outer world
you gazed at longingly,
your body not built for land
with its single powerful limb
that you asked me to split in two.
I did what my witchery could.

'To be human means to decline
in a blink of your human time.
Your walking will be pierced
as by blades that grow sharper by dark
and slice into your sleep.
For you there is never a rest
but the muffled sound of the sea
hitting the shingle bank.
There is no guarantee of love
or health or a gentle end.
The object of your desire
loved a mermaid. His human love
was younger than you and the child
who played on the beach was not yours.
You are doomed to hobble alone
through the days and the nights of the real
when you could have remained a dream.

The depths where your siblings swim
are out of your crippled reach.
You are actual cannot go back
to the myth that once you were.
My magic does not allow
an argument with time.
You have made your choice and are
as you are, a vessel for pain.

'You cannot return to the sea
unless it may be to drown.'

(2009)

ICEBERG ROSE

Like a discarded poem
on a crumpled scrap of paper
hangs the white February rose,
dirtied by winter, shredded by wet winds.

I did not know it took so long to die,

so many moaning winds
and roaring rains,
so many shapes of moon
and shades of sky,

all the long drawn-out darks,
slow-opening days,
sparkling or misted,
frosted or in cloud,

so many dusks
and winter dusk-like days
and, past their season,
lingering damaged flowers,

so many endings
long before the end.

(2010)

The carbon released in the production this book has been offset by tree planting.

The paper used complies with FSC (Forest Stewardship Council) and PEFC (Programme for the Endorsement of Forest Certification) Chain of Custody standards.

www.booksondemand-worldwide.com

www.bardicmedia.co.uk